MW00759884

To:

_____

You are a gift from God,
my sister, my friend.

From:

_____

My Sister, My Friend
Copyright 2004 by Zondervan Corporation
ISBN 0-310-80776-X

Requests for information should be addressed to:
Inspirio, The gift group of Zondervan
Grand Rapids, Michigan 49530
http://www.inspiriogifts.com

Project management and compilation: Molly C. Detweiler
Design: Kimberly Visser

Printed in China
04 05 06/HK/ 4 3 2 1

my Sister,
my Friend

inspirio™

There's a special
kind of freedom sisters enjoy.
Freedom to share
innermost thoughts,
to ask a favor,
to show their true feelings.
The freedom to
simply be themselves.

ANONYMOUS

Sisters are the people who give you a tissue, a hug and a shoulder to cry on, even when you're crying so hard that your nose gets runny.

A ministering angel shall my sister be.

WILLIAM SHAKESPEARE

Your love
has given me great joy
and encouragement.

PHILEMON 7

M ay the LORD keep watch
between you and me
when we are away from each other.

GENESIS 31:49

A sister writes
her love on your heart,
So wherever you go,
you're never apart.

MOLLY DETWEILER

I always smile when I think about you,
knowing that no matter where I go or what
I do, I will always have you on my side,
cheering for me all the way.

For there is no friend like a sister
In calm or stormy weather;
To cheer one on the tedious way,
To fetch one if one goes astray,
To lift one if one totters down,
To strengthen whilst one stands.

CHRISTINA ROSETTI

Bless you, my darling, and remember
you are always in the heart—
oh tucked so close there is no
chance of escape—of your sister.

KATHERINE MANSFIELD

Sisters are for sharing laughter
and wiping tears.

AUTHOR UNKNOWN

May kindness and
faithfulness be with you.

2 SAMUEL 15:20

My sisters have taught me how to live.

She speaks with wisdom
and faithful instruction
is on her tongue.

PROVERBS 31:26

I've learned so much from you. You taught me everything I needed to know about dressing kittens in doll clothes, making the perfect mud pie, and of course, how to accessorize!

My sister is *patient*, my sister is kind.

She does not envy when I get a job promotion or go on a nice vacation.

She does not boast when she's right and I'm wrong.

She is not proud— she never looks down on anyone.

She is not rude—she extends *kindness* and courtesy to everyone she meets.

My sister is not self-seeking— *she loves* to give and help.

My sister is not easily angered— I marvel at her patience!

She doesn't keep a record of wrongs—
I ruined her favorite sweater when we were
teenagers, but she doesn't ever bring it up.

My sister never delights in evil but rejoices
in telling the truth with love.

She always seeks to **protect** me when she can.

She **trusts** me with her secrets.

She always helps me feel hopeful
in the midst of difficult times.

She perseveres, even when things get tough.

My sister has never failed
to show me love!

1 Corinthians 13:4-8

(A sisterly paraphrase!)

Having a sister is like having a best friend you can't get rid of. You know whatever you do, she'll still be there.

AMY LI

God made us sisters,
and then, in our hearts,
made us friends.

CHRISTINA SMITH

I'm so glad that I can't ever "get rid" of you. You understand me in a way no one else can—and you love me in spite of it all! Thanks for always being there for me. I hope you know that I'll always do the same for you, my dear sister.

May the road rise to meet you.

May the wind be always
at your back.

May the sun shine
warm upon your face,

And the rain fall
soft upon your fields.

And until we meet again

May God hold you
in the palm of his hand.

IRISH BLESSING

A sister smiles when one tells one's stories for she knows where the decoration has been added.

CHRIS MONTAIGNE

We played hide and seek
for hours each day
We dressed up in Mom's clothes
and put on a play
We made so many memories,
we laughed and we cried
I'll always be thankful
I had you by my side.

MOLLY DETWEILER

There can be no situation in life
in which the conversation of my dear sister
will not administer some comfort to me.

LADY MARY WORLEY MONTAGU

When I'm feeling blue, you always
help me see things from a different angle.
What a blessing it is to have a sister who
can always show me the sunny side of life!

A sister is one who reaches
for your hand
and touches your heart.

AUTHOR UNKNOWN

A sister is a part of
your essential self, an eternal
presence of your heart and
soul and memory.

SUSAN CABILL

The best thing
about having a sister is that
I always have a friend.

CALI RAE TURNER

I love all the little inside jokes
and silly secrets we share.
It's so fun to simply give you
a smile or a wink
that will send us both into
uncontrollable giggles!

No matter what else goes on in the
world, there is nothing that a sister, two
spoons, and a carton of double chocolate
chip ice cream won't make better!

I so love the times
when we can sit together and ask,
"Do you remember...?"
Between your memories and mine
we can bring back
a whole host of good times and
have fun reliving them together.
Thanks for all our
walks down memory lane—
I look forward to many more!

There is no time like the old time,
　　　when you and I were young!

OLIVER WENDELL HOLMES

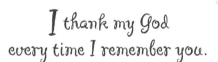

*I thank my God
every time I remember you.*

PHILIPPIANS 1:3

Some people still have their first dollar. The person who is really rich, though, is the one who still has her first friend. I am wealthy beyond compare because I have you, my first friend, my sister!

There's happiness in little things,

There's joy in passing pleasure.

But your friendship, sister,

from year to year,

Is the best of all life's treasure.

God gave me such an incredible gift when he gave you to me as my sister. I will be eternally grateful to our heavenly Father for blessing me so richly.

❧

Our brother thinks my sister
    and I have a *magical connection*.
I tell him, "Yes, we do.
    It's called the phone company!"

GRETTA BAXTER

You put the fun in together,
The sad in apart,
The hope in tomorrow,
And the joy in my heart!

Sisters touch your heart in ways no other could. Sisters share their hopes, their fears, their love, everything they have. Real friendship springs from their special bonds.

CARRIE BAGWELL

I LOVE YOU, SIS ...

You believe in me,
    even when I doubt myself.

You love me,
    even when I don't act very loveable.

You push me to do my best
    when I feel like giving up.

You let me cry on your shoulder
    whenever I need listening ear.

You love me unconditionally—
    you're my very best friend!

Oh, the comfort, the inexpressible comfort of feeling safe with a person; having neither to weigh thoughts nor measure words, but to pour them all out, just as they are, chaff and grain together, knowing that a faithful hand will take and sift them, keep what is worth keeping, and then, with the breath of kindness, blow the rest away.

MARY ANN EVANS

To the outside world we all grow old,
but not to sisters.
We know each other as we always were.
We know each other's hearts.
We share private family jokes.
We remember family feuds and secrets,
sorrows and joys.
We live outside the touch of time.

CLARA ORTEGA

TO A SPECIAL SISTER

A sister is one of the nicest things
   that can happen to anyone.

She is someone to laugh with and share with,
   to work with and join in the fun.

She is someone who helps in the rough times
   and knows when you need a warm smile.

She is someone who will quietly listen
   when you just want to talk for awhile.

A sister is dear to you always,
   for she is someone who is always a part
   of all the favorite memories
   that you keep very close to your heart.

AUTHOR UNKNOWN

Thanks for always being there
to lend a helping hand
when I really needed it.
Somehow you always know
exactly what I need the most!

Help one another,
is part of the religion of sisterhood.

LOUISA MAY ALCOTT

A kindhearted woman
gains respect.

PROVERBS 11:16

Sisters are as close as hands and feet.

ANCIENT PROVERB

Sisters—they share the agony and
the exhilaration. As youngsters they may
share popsicles, chewing gum, hair dryers,
and bedrooms. When they grow up, they
share careers, children, conversations,
and confidences.

ROXANNE BROWN

In all my prayers for… you, I always
pray with joy. … It is right for me to feel
this way about… you, since I have you
in my heart.

PHILIPPIANS 1:4, 7

There is a fellowship more quiet
even than solitude,
and which, rightly understood,
is solitude made perfect.

ROBERT LOUIS STEVENSON

M

ay the God of hope fill you
with all joy and peace as you trust in
him, so that you may overflow with
hope by the power of the Holy Spirit.

ROMANS 15:13

What's the good of news
if you haven't a sister to share it?

JENNY DEVRIES

My sister is the first person I call with
good news, so we can celebrate together.
No matter what I'm feeling, her response
is the one I want to hear before anyone
else's. She is my sounding board, my
confidante, my keeper of secrets—
and my best friend.

KATHLEEN O'KEEFE

I, who have no sisters or brothers,
   look with some degree of
   innocent envy on those who
   may be said to be born friends.

JAMES BOSWELL

What a wonderful present
God gave me when he gave me
you, who is not only my sister,
but who is also a dear friend!
There aren't enough words in the
world to express how grateful I
am for the gift of you.

Blessings for you ...

May you be blessed by the Lord,
the Maker of heaven and earth.

Psalm 115:15

The Lord bless you and keep you;
the Lord make his face shine upon you
and be gracious to you;
the Lord turn his face toward you
and give you peace.

Numbers 6:24–26

SOME WORDS OF "WISDOM" FOR YOU

Always have at least five items
with the word "fudge" in their name
in your house at any given time.
You never know when there might
be an "emergency."

Exercise is important—
walking in the mall
with a full shopping bag in each hand
is aerobics and weight training.

Laugh and
the world laughs with you—cry
and you streak your mascara.

🌿

Talk therapy is expensive——
talking to me
at ten cents a minute
is a bargain!

A sister is a gift to the heart, a
friend to the spirit, a golden thread
to the meaning of life.

ISADORA JAMES

Sensational

Interesting

Sensitive

Tender

Encouraging

Radiant

The mildest,
drowsiest sister has been known
to turn tiger if her sibling
is in trouble.

CLARA ORTEGA

I had no trouble giving you a hard time; I know I teased you mercilessly sometimes. But if someone else dared to do the same I'd give them a nice lunch of knuckle sandwich. No one picks on my sister—except me!

The unfading beauty of a
gentle and quiet spirit ...
is of great worth
in God's sight.

1 PETER 3:4

You are so beautiful, inside and out.
Your beauty shines in the way you show
love and give encouragement to all those
you meet. When people tell me that I am
a lot like you, I take that as a great
compliment!

God has made everything
beautiful in its time.

ECCLESIASTES 3:11

Siblings are the people we practice on,
the people who teach us about fairness
and cooperation and kindness and caring.

PAMELA DUGDALE

She takes my hand and
leads me along paths I would not have
dared explore alone.

MAYA V. PATEL

Many women do noble things,
but you surpass them all.

PROVERBS 31:29

Your love has helped me handle
the little ups and downs of life.
The moments that are tearful
And full of lonely strife.
And then there are the moments
Full of cheerfulness and glee;
I'm so glad your heart is furnished
With a little place for me.

DORIS RIKKERS

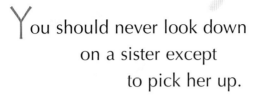

You should never look down
on a sister except
to pick her up.

AUTHOR UNKNOWN

You always make me feel special and valued,
even when I'm not at my best. Thank you for
being there to pick me up and dust me off
when I fall. I want to always be there for you
when you need me.

If one falls down, the other helps,
But if there's no one to help, tough!

ECCLESIASTES 4:10 THE MESSAGE

I'm smiling because you are my sister
and laughing because
there is nothing you can do about it.

AUTHOR UNKNOWN

Whenever I get the urge to embarrass you with a story about your botched perm in seventh grade or the time you had an "accident" while on a family vacation I remember all those stories you could tell on me. And I keep my mouth shut ... unless you're not there.

Every sister has a fund of embarrassing stories she can bring out at the most effective moment.

PAMELA DUGDALE

I know I've never told you
In the hurried rush of days
How much your friendship helps me
In a thousand little ways;
But you've played such a part
In all I do or try to be,
I want to tell you thank you
For being not just sisters,
But also friends, with me.

Write your sister's
weak points in the sand and
her strong points in stone.

AUTHOR UNKNOWN

In spite of my many faults, you
never hold them over my head.
Thanks for bringing out the best in
me while being gentle with the rest
of me!

My sister stands by
When storm clouds fly,
She's there through thick and thin.
And when I really need some help
She always steps right in.

My prayers for you, my sister, my friend ...

I pray also that the eyes of your heart may be enlightened in order that you may know the hope to which God has called you, the riches of his glorious inheritance in the saints, and his incomparably great power for us who believe.

EPHESIANS 1:18–19

This is my prayer: that your love may abound more and more in knowledge and depth of insight, so that you may be able to discern what is best and may be pure and blameless until the day of Christ, filled with the fruit of righteousness that comes through Jesus Christ—to the glory and praise of God.

PHILIPPIANS 1:9–11

I pray that out of God's glorious riches he may strengthen you with power through his Spirit in your inner being, so that Christ may dwell in your hearts through faith. And I pray that you, being rooted and established in love, may have power, together with all the saints, to grasp how wide and long and high and deep is the love of Christ, and to know this love that surpasses knowledge—that you may be filled to the measure of all the fullness of God.

EPHESIANS 3:16–19

Dear friend, I pray that
you may enjoy good health and that
all may go well with you,
even as your soul is getting along well.

3 JOHN 2

SISTERS

Sisters share a closeness
no one else can understand.

A sister's always there
to give a hug or lend a hand.

Sisters are the best friends
in the whole wide world, it's true.

And that friendship is a blessing
that lasts a lifetime through.

AUTHOR UNKNOWN

Sometimes when the skies are gray

My sister calls to brighten the day

And after we have said goodbye

The sun comes out to light my sky!

How can we thank God enough for you in return for all the joy we have in the presence of our God because of you?

1 THESSALONIANS 3:9

Grace and peace to you
    from God our Father and
    from the Lord Jesus Christ.

ROMANS 1:7

At Inspirio
we love to hear from you–

your stories, your feedback, and your product ideas.

Please send your comments to us by way of e-mail at icares@zondervan.com or to the address below:

inspirio

Attn: Inspirio Cares
5300 Patterson Avenue SE
Grand Rapids, MI 49530

If you would like further information about Inspirio and the products we create please visit us at:

www.inspiriogifts.com

Thank you and God Bless!